Contents

The Hike

"Who had this silly idea?" Latif Khan asked the others in the minibus.

"Don't ask so many questions, Latif, I'm trying to sleep,"
5 said James Fraser. "Don't you know it's only half past six?"

"Now who is asking questions?" said Sarah O'Neill from her seat at the back. "Oh, oh, oh, what am I doing here? We never got up at this time at Beacon Park."

"You're here," answered Martin Walker, "because some-
10 body at Beacon Park said, 'I know about a great adventure camp in the Lake District. Let's all meet again there next summer!' Now who was that? Do you remember, Sarah?"

"Hey, what's wrong with you all?" asked Lynn Thomas, the fifth member of the group. "We all thought it was a really
15 good idea. That's why everybody has come. Come on, it's going to be a lovely day, we're going on a beautiful hike, so be happy or be quiet."

"Some people are *always* happy," whispered James to Martin. And then: "Oh, no, I think we've arrived."

20 The minibus stopped. "Blea Tarn," called Mr Hanbury, the activity leader who was driving them. "Everybody out."

The five friends got out of the minibus into the clear Lake District morning. "Brrr, is it really August?" asked Latif. The others stood there and looked cold and unhappy.

25 "Don't worry," laughed Mr Hanbury. "You're going to get warm enough today. Now remember, you've got a hard hike, and the weather is going to be hot. So don't go too fast, you aren't in a race. Don't forget to drink enough water, and stop and eat something when you get tired. Oh,
30 and stay on the paths and roads. These mountains can be dangerous if you get lost."

Then Mr Hanbury asked, "Have you got everything? All right. You know where you're going. Over the Wrynose Pass and the Hardknott Pass and down into Eskdale. You can get

a minibus to Wast Water there. You've got the map, haven't you, Sarah? Good. I'll be at Wast Water camp site with the other group this evening, and we'll all spend the night there. Have a good time." And he got back into the minibus
5 and drove away.

They walked across the road and down to Blea Tarn, a small and lonely lake in the steep, blue-green mountains of the Lake District. The morning sun was already shining on the tops, but down by the water it was still cold.

10 "Come on, we need to move," said Lynn.

"Just a minute," said Martin. "Give me the map, Sarah, I want to look at something."

"You could say 'please'," answered Sarah, but she gave it to him.

15 "Hey, listen," said Martin. "Just what I thought. Mr Hanbury has chosen a boring hike for us. We've got to go along a road all the time. But if we go over that hill, we can climb on those rocks. And we'll still get to the Wrynose Pass later."

20 Latif looked at the hill. "There isn't a path," he said.

"No, there isn't," agreed Sarah. "Look at the map. That way is too steep and dangerous, Martin. We can never climb that – we aren't sheep! And you heard Mr Hanbury, too. Look, there's the path, along here. Let's go."

25 "Come on, James," said Martin. "We can go over the rocks together. The others can go along the boring road if they want."

"We won't wait for you," called Lynn. "And we've got the map."

30 James looked at Martin, then started to walk after the others. Martin waited a minute or two before he did the same. "Sheep," he said loudly, "are animals that always need a leader."

"What do you mean?" shouted the others. Martin didn't
35 answer.

5

They walked together along the path away from Blea Tarn, but nobody spoke. The colours of the mountains were changing all the time in the early morning light. The grass, still wet after the night, shone in the sun. Birds were singing everywhere. There were no tourists. They were alone except for a few sheep. It really was a beautiful day. The Lake District was in a sunny mood, but the five friends were not. The birds were just noisy. So were the sheep, and the silly animals were always on the path. Their jeans were wet from the grass, too. It was a terrible day.

To get from Blea Tarn to the Wrynose Pass, you've got to climb 200 metres. Most of the way is along a very steep and narrow road. When the group got to the road and looked up at the Wrynose Pass, they were in an angry mood.

"Have we really got to go up there? It's like the wall of a house!" said Martin.

"Yes, and the sun is starting to get hot. It'll be terrible," said Latif.

"What now, Martin?" said Lynn. She was still angry about his sheep 'joke'. "Half an hour ago you wanted to go rock-climbing with James up a really steep hill. And you said it was too cold, Latif. Is nothing right for you? Now we can all climb and we can all get hot. Isn't that enough for you? I'm on holiday, and I don't want to spend it with people in a bad mood about nothing. I'm going to walk to Eskdale. Come if you want, or stay here all day."

"I'm going with Lynn," said Sarah, "and I'm taking the map. If you don't come with us, you can try and find your way back to the camp without it."

Slowly they all began to climb up to Wrynose. It got harder and harder, and hotter and hotter. Latif tried to enjoy the mountains all around him, but he couldn't. He looked down at the road and walked. He started to talk: "I – am – en – joy – ing – this. – I – am – hav – ing – fun," he said again and again.

The others heard him and began to smile. Then they started to laugh, and suddenly their bad mood just went. Almost before they knew it, they were at the top.

They ran off the road and up a few rocks, and they could see for miles. "Hey, look at that," said James. "All that climbing was worth it. And from now on, it's easy. We've done the hardest part of the hike already."

Sarah had the map, and she knew James was wrong. But she didn't want the bad mood back, so she only said, "Here's just the right place for a late breakfast."

The walk down from Wrynose Pass to Wrynose Bottom was very different from the walk up. They felt happier, they could walk and enjoy the wild colours of the mountains at the same time, and they talked. They talked about Beacon Park and made plans for the Lake District.

The River Duddon goes through Wrynose Bottom, and the path goes along the river. They stopped for a few minutes and washed their feet in the cold water. "Mmmm, this is sooo good," said Lynn. "I never want to wear shoes again."

"The water is good to drink, too," said James. "Try some."

"No thanks, James!" said Sarah. "Haven't you seen those sheep there? What do you think they're doing in the water?"

7

"Uuuuugh, oh no! And I've drunk it!" shouted James. "Why didn't you tell me? And what are you all laughing at? I don't think it's funny!"

When they started again, James walked alone, behind the others. "Real friends tell you before you drink … uuugh. I don't want to think about it, and I don't want to talk to them."

Everybody except James enjoyed the flat, easy walk by the Duddon. When they got to the lonely house at Cockley Beck bridge, Martin and Latif turned left, to stay with the river.

"Hey," called Sarah. "Where are you two going? Come back. We've got to go right here."

Martin and Latif turned – and then they saw the road up to Hardknott Pass. From Wrynose Bottom up to Hardknott Pass you've got to climb 200 metres in about one and a half kilometres. It's the steepest road in the Lake District, and perhaps in all England.

"You two aren't fair!" shouted Martin. "You knew about that from the map and you didn't tell us. We'll never get up there. It's so hot now, and I've drunk all my water."

James didn't miss his chance to laugh. "No problem, Martin," he said. "Just fill your water bottle from the river." And he started up the hill.

"Sorry, Martin," said Sarah. "I didn't mean it like that, really." Then she and Lynn went off after James. Latif, too. "Hey, not so fast," shouted Martin. "Give me that map. *I* want it now!" But the others didn't stop.

It took a long time and a lot of hard work to get to the top, and this time Latif couldn't get them into a good mood. Martin was still angry with Sarah and Lynn, and James was still angry with everybody. But from the top, they could see Eskdale and, a long way away, the sea; and behind them were still the wild, beautiful mountains of the Lake District.

"Oh, wow!" said Latif. "Have we come up all that way? I've never climbed anything like that. I'm going to write my name and the date on that rock over there. Then everybody will know!" And he found a hard stone and ran over to
5 some big rocks.

"Good idea, me too," shouted James, and ran after him.

"Hey, no!" shouted Martin. "That's a silly idea. Come on, they mustn't do that. We've got to stop them." And the other three ran to the rocks, too.

10 Latif and James looked at their friends in surprise.

"What's wrong? It's a great idea. Come on, we can all write our names. It'll look good."

"It'll look terrible," said Martin. "Everything is so beautiful up here. Why do you want to spoil it?"

15 "Yes, and what's great about it?" asked Sarah. "So Latif Khan and James Fraser were here. But nobody wants to know that."

"Well, we want to tell them," answered James. "And what do you mean 'spoil'? You can't spoil all these mountains
20 with just two names on one rock."

"That's right," agreed Latif. "And it's important to *me*. I'll know my name is up here. You don't need to write your names if you don't want to."

"Listen," answered Martin. "Just two names, you said, OK?
25 But if you start, other people will do it, too. Think about it. What's it going to look like here if there are a hundred names? Or two hundred? Or more? And who is going to see your names then?"

"Please, Latif," said Sarah.

30 Latif looked at his feet. "Oh, all right," he said, and threw his stone away. James looked at the others and then did the same. He and Latif started to walk down to Eskdale. They didn't wait for the other three.

Eskdale is very different from the wild parts of the Lake
35 District. Everywhere is green, and under the trees it isn't so

hot. It's easy to walk the paths and roads along the River Esk, and the five friends were glad to be there after their long walk through the mountains. They were tired now and looking forward to getting a Mountain Goat minibus to Wast Water.

"The first village is called Boot," said Lynn. "I'm sure we'll get a bus there."

But before they got to Boot, they saw a sign to Dalegarth Station.

"A station? Here?" said Martin. "That's strange."

Just then, they heard a whistle. "Steam trains!" shouted Sarah. "Come on, let's go and look."

They ran to the station and stopped, disappointed when they saw the train. "It's only a toy train," said Sarah. "It probably just goes half a mile and back again."

"No, no," said Lynn, who was reading the station notice board. "It says here 'Ravenglass and Eskdale Railway', and the trains go all the way to Ravenglass. Hey, Ravenglass. That's on the coast. We can take the train and go and swim in the sea!"

But to her surprise, not everybody thought that was a good idea. Sarah wanted to go to the sea. Latif wasn't sure. Martin wanted to go to Wast Water because it was late and he was tired. James wanted to go to Wast Water because he was still angry with everybody. Lynn put her head in her hands.

"What's wrong with us all?" she asked. "We say we're friends, but we can't agree about anything. We've had argument after argument, all day. Now come on, please. We've got lots of time, it's only half past three. Let's have an easy trip on a steam train and then go swimming in the sea. It'll do us good after our hard hike."

In summer, the trains on the Ravenglass and Eskdale are open. It was just what the five needed after their long, hot walk. They could feel the warm wind in their hair as the

train went through the woods and fields of Eskdale, away
from the roads and then along the River Mite to Ravenglass.
It felt good.
Ravenglass is a small village where the River Mite goes into
the sea. "Race you to the water!" shouted Lynn, when they
got off the train, and they all ran towards the coast.
"Well," said James, when they stopped. "We can choose.
Do we want to swim in the river, or in the sea?"
"Or both," said Martin, who wasn't tired any more.
Just then, a woman who was watching them came over.
"Did you say 'swim'?" she asked. And then: "It really isn't a
good idea to swim here."
The five looked at her in surprise.
"Yes," she said. "We're only a few miles away from a place
called Sellafield."
"Sellafield!" said Sarah. "Oh, no! We know about Sellafield
in Ireland. That's where that nuclear reprocessing plant is."
"That's right," said the woman. "And nobody really knows
what they put in the water. So I wouldn't like to swim in the
sea here. Or in the river. The sea water goes a long way up."
There was nothing to say. They walked through the lovely
village, but they couldn't enjoy it. They were all in a sad and
angry mood – different from the bad mood of the morning.
"It's so beautiful here," said Martin. "It doesn't look dangerous."
They took the train back, and got off at Eskdale Green for
the Mountain Goat bus to Wast Water. "Oh well," said
Lynn. "At last we've found something that we all agree
about. But it hasn't made us happy."
Wast Water did that. It's the loneliest, most beautiful lake
in the Lake District. When they saw it, they stopped
thinking about Sellafield. On one side is the narrow road,
on the other, the steep, blue mountains go down into the
water. And at the camp site, you can swim in the lovely,
cold water of the lake.

11

It's Hotter There

"Mountains again!"

"What do you mean, James?" asked one of the others.

"I mean it's the same every day. Every time I get up in this
camp, there are mountains everywhere. It never changes.
I'd love to see a few nice flat fields."

"This is bad, James," said Martin. "I think you've got
mountainitis. You're going to have to go back home early."

"That isn't going to help him," said Latif. "Scotland is all
mountains."

"That just shows you've never been to Scotland, Latif,"
answered James. "Around Aberdeen, everywhere is quite
flat. The mountains are miles away. You still think Scottish
people don't like to spend money, don't you?"

"No, of course not!" said Latif. "How can you ...?" He
stopped, because the others were laughing.

"It's all right, Latif," said Sarah. "It's just another of James's
jokes. He loves mountains, really, and he's glad he's here
and not in the cold north."

"Cold north! In Aberdeen, you can cook eggs on the road in
summer," laughed James. "But come on, what are we going
to do today? How many mountains are we going to climb
before lunch?"

"You climb them," said Latif, "and we can stay here and
watch. It's much too hot, today. Can't we just stay here and
look at the beautiful mountains?"

"Lazybones," laughed Lynn. "Over to the camp centre with
you. Activities. That's what we need."

They were looking at the notice board when Mr Mosley,
one of the activity leaders came past. "Everything OK?" he
asked. And then: "Hey Latif, why are you down there on the
floor?"

"Because it's too hot to stand," answered Latif.

12

"Oh, come on, it's much hotter than this where you come from!" laughed Mr Mosley, and he went out.

But Latif didn't laugh. The others were talking loudly about all the different activities, when one of them looked at Latif in surprise.

"What's wrong with you, Latif?" he asked. "You're suddenly very quiet."

"Did you hear him?" asked Latif.

"Who?"

"Mr Mosley. 'It's much hotter where you come from'. Did you hear that?"

"Well, perhaps it is," laughed James. "What's the weather like in Halifax? Did you phone home yesterday?"

"Oh, be quiet, James," said Sarah. "Can't you see? Latif is upset."

"He thinks I'm not British," said Latif, angry now. "For him I'm just a Paki!"

"Oh, no, I'm sure that isn't right," said Lynn. "Mr Mosley is too nice. He didn't want to say that."

"Well, what did he want to say then?" shouted Latif.

"He probably didn't want to say anything," said Martin. "It was just a joke. Like when you said 'Scotland is all mountains'."

"A joke?" said Sarah. "Well, who is laughing? And Latif didn't say anything about Scottish *people* and money."

"Yes, but ... oh, it isn't important," said James. "Look, I hear Scottish jokes all the time. So what. They're always the same, they're just boring. You don't need to get angry and spoil the day because of something like that. That's silly."

"Oh," shouted Latif. "So I'm silly, am I? And I'm spoiling your day? You don't understand anything, do you? Well, if I'm not here, perhaps you can all enjoy your day!" And he ran out.

"Great, James," said Sarah. "That was really good. There are probably enough people in Halifax who call Latif a 'Paki'.

13

He doesn't need to hear things like that on holiday, too. And he doesn't need friends who say it isn't important. I'm going to try to find him." And she went out after him.

Sarah looked everywhere in the camp for Latif, but she couldn't find him. "He has gone off somewhere alone," she told the others. "I hope he's all right."

The others looked down at their feet and didn't say anything. At last Martin spoke, "It's all our fault, isn't it?" he said. "I mean, we didn't really think. We just don't have that problem. If somebody talks to us about 'where we come from', they never mean 'you don't belong in this country'. We don't know what it's like."

The four spent most of the day in the camp. There were enough interesting activities for them, but they couldn't really enjoy them.

At eight o'clock in the evening, Latif still wasn't back. "Where can he be?" asked Lynn. "Perhaps something has happened to him."

"Well, we mustn't wait any more," said James. "We've got to tell the activity leaders."

They found Mr Mosley. "What?" he shouted, when they told him. "You say he went at half past nine and you've waited till now? Why didn't you tell somebody earlier? And nobody knows where he has gone? Oh no! Come with me. I've got to tell the other activity leaders, and phone the police and the mountain rescue. We've got to find him – but where can we start to look? He could be anywhere!"

When Latif ran out of the camp centre, he just wanted to get away. He didn't have any ideas about where. He ran out of the camp, saw a Mountain Goat minibus and got on. The bus didn't take him very far. It only went to Coniston, a small town – or big village – by Coniston Water, one of the biggest lakes in the Lake District.

"Now what do I do?" he thought. He wasn't quite so upset now, but he was still very, very angry. "I know," he thought.

14

"If I buy a map, I can find a way up into the mountains. The tourists don't go up there. It's too much hard work for them."

Latif bought a map and some bread and cheese. He found a
5 path that went up a mountain called The Old Man of Coniston and started to walk. "I don't need to go to the top," he thought. "If I go half way, I'll see all of the lake. Then I can sit and have my picnic. That'll be nice."

He walked for about an hour and a half. He stopped often
10 to listen to the birds or look at the view. This got better with every metre he climbed. Quite a few other people were hiking along the path. They said hallo to him, or gave him a friendly smile, and so his mood began to get better, too.

The climb was hard in the hot sun. So when he stopped,
15 Latif was quite tired.

"Ahhh, this is the place for a picnic," he said. "The view is terrific." He walked away from the path, dropped onto the grass, and went to sleep in the sun.

Three hours later, a big black sheep found Latif. Sheep are
20 always interested in things that they find strange. This one stood behind Latif's head and said "baaaa", very loudly.

"Aaaaaaaagh," shouted Latif, and jumped up. The sheep ran a few metres, then stopped and watched him. "Whew, was I shocked!" said Latif. "And what am I doing here?"
25 Then he remembered everything.

"You're the only black sheep here," he said to the sheep. "Do they call you 'Paki', too?" Then he started to laugh. "Now I'm getting very, very silly," he thought. "And it was silly to be so angry with the others this morning. It isn't
30 their fault if they don't know what it's like. They don't think I belong in Pakistan. And Mr Mosley isn't the only activity leader. I haven't got to do things together with him."

15

Latif ate his bread and cheese, with some help from his sheep. Then he sat for a long time and looked at the beautiful view over Coniston Water. He felt quite happy when he at last walked slowly back down to Coniston.

5 It was past seven o'clock when Latif got back to Coniston. "So late!" he thought. "I forgot about the time. I hope there's still a bus out to the camp."
The next bus wasn't till nine o'clock. "Hmm, we've always got to be back in the camp at nine o'clock," he thought.
10 "Oh well, I can walk. It isn't so very far."

Mr Mosley put the phone down. "Well, the police are going to look for him. The mountain rescue are going to try to do something, too. But it's going to be dark in an hour or so, and they don't know where to start."
15 "Why didn't he tell anybody?" asked Ms Aston, one of the other leaders. "If he's somewhere up in the mountains, he'll probably be there all night, now."
Sarah looked at the door. "Latif!" she said.
"Hallo," said Latif, and smiled.
20 "Where have you been, you stupid boy?" shouted Mr

16

Mosley. "Don't you know …" He didn't get any further.

"Don't you shout at him," Sarah shouted at Mr Mosley. "It's all your fault, you with your nasty jokes! That's why Latif went away."

5 Mr Mosley looked shocked. "Nasty jokes?" he said.

"Yes," shouted Sarah. "We all heard you. 'It's much hotter than this where you come from.' That's what you said. Well, he doesn't come from Pakistan, Mr Mosley. He comes from Halifax. He was born there. He's British, like you and 10 me."

It was very quiet in the room. Nobody spoke, and nobody moved. At last Mr Mosley said, "I've got to phone the police and the mountain rescue, and tell them everything is OK." When he put the phone down, he looked at Latif, and said, 15 "I'm sorry, Latif. I've got to learn to think before I speak. And I'm sorry I shouted and called you stupid. That was because I was very worried about you."

Latif didn't know what to answer. So he said nothing and tried to smile.

20 "Come on, let's have some tea," said Ms Aston. "It's easier to talk with a cup in your hand. And I'm sure Latif needs something to eat and drink."

Latif agreed.

"Good idea," said Mr Mosley, too, and he looked happier.

25 "Er…, Mr Mosley," said Latif. "I'm sorry, too, erm…, I mean, I didn't think. You know, about the police and the mountain rescue and that …"

"Hmmm," said Ms Aston, "we've got quite a problem in this camp with people who don't think, haven't we? Oh 30 well, everything is all right now. But remember one thing. If you go out of the camp alone, tell somebody where you're going. And if you forget, because you're upset and angry," – now she looked at Latif – "then use the phone – please! OK?"

35 "OK," came the answer.

The Fell Race

"Did you know that William Wordsworth lived in Grasmere?" asked Lynn, one evening. "That isn't far from here."

5 "No, I didn't," answered Martin, who was eating a big bag of chips. "How do you know? Did he write his name on a rock or something?"

"Oh, really, Martin!" said Sarah. "Wordsworth is one of England's most famous poets. He wrote lots of beautiful 10 poems about the Lake District and about other parts of England."

"Did he really?" answered Martin. "Here, have a chip."

"I'll have one, too," said James. "Mmm, they're good. Now, what are we going to do tomorrow? It's a free day. We 15 haven't got to do any camp activities if we don't want to. We can do anything we like."

Sarah put her head in her hands, Lynn looked hard at the two boys. "Sometimes," she said, very slowly, "I would like to drop rocks on your heads. Tomorrow, we can go to 20 Grasmere and visit Wordsworth's house."

"Oh, no, how boring!" said James and Martin together. "Poets are for school. We're on holiday here."

"Aren't you two interested in anything except mountains and chips?" asked Lynn. "The house is a lovely museum. 25 It's called Dove Cottage. Wordsworth lived there almost 200 years ago, and it's still just like it was then. They haven't changed anything. Sarah and I are interested in seeing that."

"I've got an idea," said Martin. "Let's see. How many of us 30 want to visit a dead poet, and how many want to do something interesting? Hands up."

"You can forget that, Martin," said James. "If Sarah wants to go to Wordsworth's house, then Latif will go, too. Those

18

two are always together now, so that's three to two – aren't I right?" he asked.

Sarah went red. Latif just laughed and said, "That isn't really fair. I'm interested in Wordsworth and in old houses,
5 too. And you haven't got to come with us. You two can do something different, if you want."

So the next day, they all went to Grasmere together.

Grasmere is one of the smaller lakes in the Lake District. The village by the lake, where Wordsworth had his house,
10 is called Grasmere, too. When he lived there, from 1799 to 1813, Grasmere was a popular place with English poets. They came there because Wordsworth told them it was so beautiful and quiet. He said it gave him his best ideas. He wouldn't like Grasmere today. But he could perhaps write
15 beautiful poems about cars and coaches and thousands of tourists.

"I'm glad we're going to Grasmere on a Thursday," said Lynn in the bus. "There are fewer people there than at the weekend."
20 Just then, the bus stopped. "Are you sure?" laughed James. "Look at all these cars. The bus can't get any further."

The bus took half an hour for the last two miles into Grasmere. "It's the Grasmere Sports meeting," the driver told them. "It's the same every year on this Thursday. We
25 get twenty or thirty thousand people. Pity they don't all come by bus."

"Twenty or thirty thousand people?" said Sarah. "Oh, no!"

"Grasmere Sports?" said James. "Hey, that's great. But why do so many people come? What's special about them?"
30 "Oh, they're very famous," said the driver. "People come from everywhere to watch old Lake District sports."

"Right, first Wordsworth's house, then the Sports. That's what we agreed," said Latif, before James or Martin could say anything.

19

But when they got to Dove Cottage, there were about a hundred people outside. They were all waiting to get in. Lynn was very disappointed, but she said, "Let's not wait. It isn't going to be like 1800 with all those people in there.
5 And we can come again another day."

"Perhaps," laughed James. He and Martin weren't very sad about it. They were looking forward to the sports meeting. In the bus back to the camp, later, they couldn't stop talking about Grasmere Sports.

10 "I thought the wrestling was great," said Martin.

"Me, too," agreed Sarah. "It wasn't like the silly games that they call wrestling on TV, was it? You know, with big men who go 'uurngh, uurngh', and fall on the floor all the time."

"No," laughed Latif, "it was very different. But I don't really
15 like fighting. What about that dog race? Did you like that?" he asked.

"Was it a race?" asked James. "I thought it was something to do with hunting."

"Yes, it was," agreed Martin. "But there were prizes for
20 something. I didn't really understand everything, but it was lovely to watch."

"Mmm, yes," said Lynn. "All those beautiful dogs. But I liked the fell race best. Just think! Running all the way up that steep mountain and back down again. We had
25 problems when we *walked* up the Hardknott Pass."

"Oh well, you don't need to worry about it," said James. "You've got to be really fit and strong for a fell race. It isn't a race for girls."

"James," said Lynn. "How old are you?"
30 "Almost fourteen. Why?"

"Because my grandfather says things like that. He's eighty-four. Not a race for girls? Where *did* you find an old idea like that?"

Sarah laughed. "He has got a head full of cobwebs, and he
35 calls them ideas," she said.

20

Like lots of boys, Martin and Latif really agreed with James, but they stayed quiet. Things were getting too dangerous for them. For James, it was too late to stop.

"It isn't an old idea," he said. "There are some things that
5 girls can't do. Everybody knows that. They aren't strong enough. You just don't want to agree."

"James Fraser," answered Lynn. "If you and me ever have a fell race, you won't win it. But we'll never know, because you don't dare! Really! Are you sure you aren't eighty-four
10 and not fourteen?"

The argument didn't stop when they arrived back at the camp. Because they were so noisy, Mr Hanbury and Ms Morgan, two of the activity leaders came over.

First they listened, then they began to laugh. "All right,"
15 said Ms Morgan. "There's one way to finish this argument. We'll have a race up and down the fell behind the camp."

"Yes," agreed Mr Hanbury. "You're all quite fit now after your hikes and orienteering and so on, so a small fell race will be OK. It'll probably be quite a popular idea with the
20 others in the camp, too. If James is right, Lynn, you and the other girls won't get to the top. And if Lynn is right, James," – he laughed again – "you won't even start. Look at the notice board tomorrow."

"One, two, three, go!" shouted Mr Hanbury, and twenty
25 boys and girls from the camp started the long, difficult race up the fell. James Fraser was already running hard. He looked up at the fell. He could just see the top. It was much lower than the fell for the Grasmere race, but it was still very, very steep.

30 "Why did I start this?" James thought. "I'm like Mr Mosley. I've got to learn to think before I speak. Of course girls can run fell races. Why did I say something so stupid? And why did I say it to Lynn? She's so nice. Perhaps I said something stupid because I didn't dare to tell her I like her. Now she's

laughing at me. Half the camp laughed at me all weekend.
And, of course, every girl in the race is trying to beat me. Oh
well, I hope I finish. If I don't I really will look very silly."
He looked for Lynn, but he couldn't see her. He began to
5 run even harder.

Lynn could see James. She wasn't far behind him. "He
forgot that I do a lot of swimming and other sports in
Swansea," she thought. "This race is going to be hard, but I
can finish it, no problem. Poor James. Everybody laughed
10 at him all weekend. Even those boys who really agree with
him laughed. I hate that. It's nasty. But he has got to learn.
He mustn't think stupid things like that about girls. It's a
pity. I always thought he was very nice. Oh well, I hope he
finishes. It'll be very bad for him if he doesn't."
15 Latif was having problems. "I'm glad they started the race
at eight o'clock," he thought. "It isn't so hot. But oh, it's so
steep. Am I still running, or am I only walking? I don't
know. I see this fell every morning when I get up. I always

thought it was beautiful, like a friend. It isn't very friendly now. It's going to kill me."

Latif got slower and slower till, suddenly, he stopped and sat on the grass. "Oh well, I'm not the first one who stopped
5 running," he thought. "There are three others down there. Aaah. That's better. Now I can enjoy the view for a few minutes and then walk back down. Oh, my poor old legs. Next time I'll watch the race from the camp, like Sarah. She had the right idea."

10 Only ten got to the half way point of the race at the top of the fell. Four of them were girls. "Now comes the easy part," thought James. "Now I can really run fast."

"Be careful!" called Ms Aston, who was waiting for the runners at the top. "It isn't easy to stop when you're
15 running down a steep hill. I don't want any broken legs or sprained ankles."

"Wow," thought Lynn. "Ms Aston is right. I *can't* stop. Here we go! I hope nothing happens." She was running very fast now, passing everybody, trying hard not to fall. "Help," she
20 thought. "I'm going to win the race like this, or I'm going to break my leg. I didn't know my legs could move so fast!"

When Lynn went past him, James went after her. "We're mad," he thought. "We're going too fast. This is the end of the holiday. Hospital, here we come."

25 They were first and second now, the others far behind them. They came to the end of the steep part, and were much happier. It wasn't so dangerous. There wasn't far to go.

"Lynn," called James. "Lynn, I'm sorry!"

30 Lynn looked back at him and smiled. She ran more slowly, waited. "Come on," she said. "Let's go in together."

Helvellyn

"I love these early mornings in summer. There's nobody around. Everywhere is wet and clean after the night. The sun is shining, but it isn't too hot. I can't understand people who stay in bed. They miss the best part of the day."

"Are you all right, Martin?" asked Lynn. "You aren't ill, are you? You don't feel sick or anything?"

"No, why?" said Martin in surprise. The others in the minibus were all smiling.

"Oh, I was just thinking about the things that you said on the way to the Wrynose Pass. But perhaps I've remembered it wrong. Perhaps it was somebody else."

"Oh, the Wrynose Pass. We weren't so fit then. It was too soon. But now, it's seven o'clock in the morning, we're going to hike up one of the highest mountains in the Lake District, and I'm looking forward to it."

This time, the five were part of a bigger group from the camp. They were on their way to climb Helvellyn, a mountain 950 metres high. People from other countries often think there aren't really any mountains in Britain. "600 metres? 900 metres? Those are just hills. 2000 metres and higher – that's a mountain!"

This is a bad mistake. British mountains *are* much lower than mountains in, for example, Germany. But they're wild and difficult, and can be very, very dangerous. And that's what Ms Morgan told the group the evening before the hike: "You've got to be careful on Helvellyn. It isn't an easy hike, and there are parts which can be dangerous. Oh, and I hope you all feel fit. We've got 800 metres to climb from the lake to the top. OK, see you in the morning. We'll leave at quarter to seven in two minibuses, and Mr Mosley and I are going to be the leaders."

"Eight hundred metres," said Latif, looking up at Helvellyn. "That's a long way up."

"Don't think about it," said Sarah. "Enjoy the view over the lake."

They were at Glenridding, a village by Ullswater, the second biggest lake in the Lake District, and they were having breakfast by the water

"I'm not thinking about it," said Latif. "My legs are. They can still remember the fell race."

"Well, you haven't got to run this time," smiled Mr Mosley. "Not just haven't got to, you mustn't run. But it's time to go. Come on everybody." They all got up and walked through Glenridding to the path.

They weren't far outside the village when they first saw the dog. It was big, black and white, and friendly. Too friendly. It ran to the group and jumped up at Sarah. "Oh, get down, you stupid animal," she said. "You've got wet mud on your feet. Oh, no. Look at my clothes!"

"It isn't the animal that's stupid," said Ms Morgan. "It's the owner. I really don't like this. A dog that's running free when there are sheep around. Here, boy. Come on. Good dog."

She got the dog by the collar and looked at the address. "Just what I thought," she said. "An address in Manchester. Town people – and a town dog – who don't know how to behave in the countryside."

Martin, who was further on than the others, called back, "Ms Morgan, Mr Mosley, there are some people over here. Perhaps the dog belongs to them."

It was a family, a boy and a girl with their parents. "Oh, hallo," said the mother. "I see you've brought Bobby back. But you didn't need to. He always comes back sometime. He likes running around alone here. He can't do that in Manchester."

"I'm sure he can't," answered Ms Morgan. "And it's the same here. He can't run around alone. There are sheep here."

25

"What has that got to do with it?" asked the man.

"Dogs chase sheep," explained Ms Morgan. "Farmers in the Lake District lose lots of animals that way every year."

"Well, perhaps some dogs chase sheep," answered the mother. "But you needn't worry about our Bobby. He has never hurt anybody or anything. He's a good dog. Aren't you, boy?"

Ms Morgan tried not to be angry. "Yes, even your Bobby," she said. "He's a town dog. You don't know what he'll do in the countryside."

"Oh, now you're just being silly," said the man. "Come on, Gary, Marcia, there are too many people here."

"Er…, I hope you're going to take those things with you," said Mr Mosley, and pointed to some plastic bags and a broken bottle.

"Oh yes?" said the man. "Why do you hope that?"

"Because broken glass can hurt people and animals, and it can start grass fires in this weather," answered Mr Mosley. "And if a sheep eats one of those bags, it'll be dead in twenty-four hours."

"You've got something about sheep, haven't you?" said the woman. "Gary, Marcia, come on. We're going."

Latif and Martin started to pick up the bags and broken glass and put them in Martin's rucksack.

"Hey, Dad," said the boy called Gary. "That Paki and the other one are picking up our rubbish! They're going to take it with them."

"Yeah, some people are like that, son," answered his father, loudly. "Dirty."

"Don't you call him a Paki," shouted Sarah. "You nasty, stupid …"

"Leave it, Sarah, it's OK," said Latif. "People like that don't worry me. You can't talk to them."

"That's right," agreed Ms Morgan. "Come on, everybody. They mustn't spoil our day. Let's enjoy Helvellyn. Are you

OK with that rubbish in there, Martin? Are you sure the glass isn't going to cut you?"

All of the young people from the camp had something to say about Bobby and his family, of course. First they were all angry, but after a time, they began to feel good about the argument, in a strange way. "We" – the group from the camp – were right. "We" knew how to behave in the countryside. "They" – the family – were wrong. And nasty and stupid, too. All this made the steep climb up Helvellyn much easier. It meant that the members of the group began to make new friends, too. They talked to other boys and girls that they didn't know before.

The last part of the hike to the top of Helvellyn goes along Striding Edge. Here the path gets narrower and narrower till it's really only rocks. The two activity leaders stopped the group just before Striding Edge. The view was terrific: the steep sides of Helvellyn, and on the right, a long way down but still high in the mountains, a dark lake, Red Tarn.

"OK," said Mr Mosley. "You can see where we've got to go, and you can see what it's like. Please walk one behind the other and take it slowly. Don't look at the view too much. I know it's great, but you've got to watch where you're putting your feet. The sides of Striding Edge are very steep, and it's a long way down. If you fall, there isn't much that we can do to help you."

Out on Striding Edge, there was a strong wind. It was coming from the side, and made things more difficult. On the last part of the Edge, where the path was narrowest, they could already see the top of the mountain, quite near. Even after, Martin never really knew how it happened. One minute he was walking along and saying, "Not far, now," to the girl behind him. The next, his feet went from under him and he was falling over the side.

"Help," he shouted. Then suddenly he stopped falling. "Quick," she said. "I've got your shirt. Give me your hand."

Three or four others were quickly there and pulled Martin back onto the path. "Are you all right, Martin?" called Ms Morgan, worried. Martin couldn't speak.

"Yeah, he's OK. Just shocked, I think," the girl shouted
5 back. Then she said to Martin, "We mustn't stay here. Can you get to the end?" And she helped him to get up.

At the end of Striding Edge, there's some very easy rock-climbing to the top of Helvellyn. Everybody stood around Martin. "It's OK, I'm all right now," he said. "But I never
10 want to do that again."

"Thanks," he said to the girl. "You were very quick."

"I'm glad your shirt is so strong," she answered, and smiled at him.

The group spent half an hour at the top of Helvellyn and ate
15 their lunch. The activity leaders explained the countryside. "The lake down there to the east is Ullswater, of course, where we started from," said Ms Morgan. "And that other big lake on the west side is Thirlmere. They take the water from there for Manchester. That's about a hundred miles
20 away."

"Mmm," said Sarah. "I never want to leave here."

"Oh, just think of the cold, windy nights," laughed Lynn. "That'll help you. Come on, the others are all getting up. I think we're going to leave now."

25 To get back, they first walked down a steep path to Red Tarn. From there, they took a path along Red Tarn Beck, the stream that goes from Red Tarn down through Glenridding to Ullswater.

Suddenly Lynn said, "Hey, isn't that that Bobby over there?
30 What's the stupid dog doing up here?"

"He's chasing sheep, that's what he's doing," shouted James. "Look!" And they saw three or four sheep that were running like mad and jumping over rocks. Bobby was running hard after them.

"Come on," said Mr Mosley. "Let's hurry up. We've got to tell somebody about this."

Five minutes later, they met a man coming up the path. He was carrying a gun and he was angry.

5 "Have you got a dog with you?" he shouted. "Because there's a dog around here that's chasing my sheep. And if I get my hands on it and its owner, I'll ..."

"No, it isn't our dog," answered James. "But we know where it is." And he told the man where to look for Bobby. "
10 Hurry," he said. "Those sheep were really frightened."

Ms Morgan came over. "Here," she said to the farmer. "We've met that dog already today. This is the address of the owner, and that's our address."

"Thanks very much," said the farmer. "That's a big help.
15 Now I'm going to get after him. And when I find him ..."
The farmer started running up the path.

"Is he going to shoot Bobby?" asked Latif.

"Probably," answered Mr Mosley. "If he finds him."

"Oh, no," said Sarah. "He can't do that."

20 "Oh yes he can," said Ms Morgan. "A farmer can always

shoot a dog that chases his sheep. It's very sad, of course, because it isn't the dog's fault. But you can't shoot the owner. Sometimes, I think that's a pity!"

Back in Glenridding, Mr Mosley and Ms Morgan went for a cup of coffee together. The boys and girls walked around the village or washed their feet in the cold water of the lake. Then they bought postcards and things to eat in the village shop, and sat under the trees to write and eat.

After about an hour, they were just getting ready to go back to the camp, when a car drove into the village and stopped. Four people got out.

"Hey, it's that terrible family from this morning," said Martin. "They're probably looking for their dog."

At almost the same time, a small van with two men in it stopped outside the shop. One of them was the sheep farmer. In the back of the van, they could see Bobby.

"Hey you!" shouted the father. "What are you doing with our dog? We've spent all afternoon looking for him."

"Ah," said the farmer. "It's your dog, is it? That's good. I'll tell you what I'm doing with him. I'm taking him to the police-station."

"The police-station?" said the mother. "What for? There's no need for that. He's our dog. Our name and address is on his collar."

"Oh, I know that," answered the farmer. "But if you want him back, you can explain to the police why he was chasing my sheep up on the fells. They'll be very interested. One more thing. That address is very useful, because you're going to get a bill for two dead sheep and for the time I've spent chasing your dog this afternoon."

The farmer walked over to the group from the camp. "Thanks again for your help," he said. "It's Grasmere Sheepdog Trials next week. If you're interested, you can be my guests. Come and watch me with my dog. She's the best. I'll send some free tickets over to the camp."

You Get What You Deserve

"If those boys are eighteen, I'll eat my hat," said the man in the garden of a pub in Coniston.

"You haven't got a hat," said his wife. "But of course they
5 aren't eighteen. They aren't even sixteen. What are they doing in here without an adult?"

"They're drinking beer, that's what they're doing. But which stupid person bought it for them?"

"Hey, Martin," said James. "That man and woman are
10 looking at us. Do you think they'll tell somebody?"

"Don't look at them," answered Martin. "Perhaps they'll find something else to talk about and forget us. Come on, enjoy your beer."

"Oh, well, we can't get into trouble, can we? We're too
15 young. They can take our beer away and say 'Don't do it again,' but that's all."

"What about Willie?" asked Martin.

"Oh him," answered James. "He's gone. He went soon after he bought us the beer. And we can't tell them anything

31

about him, because we don't know anything. So he can't get into trouble."

"Perhaps not. But the owner of the pub can get into big trouble. And we don't want that, because he's one of our best friends," said the man and woman from the other table who were now standing just behind them.

"But we're only drinking a beer," said Martin.

"That's the problem," answered the woman. "You're drinking a beer in a pub garden, and you're much too young. Now come on. Get up and get out of here. And you needn't think you can't get into trouble. If you're already thirteen or fourteen, you can."

"Come on, Martin," said James. "Let's go. We've almost finished our beer." He drank some more from his glass and got up.

"Why couldn't they leave us in peace? We weren't doing anything to them," said Martin when they were outside.

"Oh, adults are like that. They always think they know better. That's why some of them are teachers," answered James. "Hey, did you like your beer?"

"I think so. But it was strong. I feel quite funny. What about you? Did you like it?"

"Hmm," said James. "Come on, let's get back to the camp. What time is it?"

"Half past eight. Let's hope there's a bus. We've got to be back in camp at nine o'clock or there'll be trouble."

There was no bus from Coniston to the camp till nine o'clock, so it was half past nine when they arrived.

"We're too late, of course," said Martin. "But if we go to the back of the camp and climb in, perhaps nobody will see us."

"Are you over, James?" whispered Martin.

"Yes," James whispered back.

"OK. Here I come."

"Good evening, James, good evening, Martin," said Ms Aston. "Now, why did you choose this interesting way to get back into the camp? Did the time have anything to do with it?" she laughed.

Then suddenly she stopped smiling at them. "Which pub were you in?"

5 "Er... pub? Erm... how do you know?" said James.

"It isn't very difficult, James," answered Ms Aston. "Beer is quite a smelly drink. Right. I want to see both of you in the camp centre tomorrow morning at half past eight. And you won't be late if you know what's good for you."

10 "But we can't," answered Martin. "We're going riding with all the others at eight o'clock."

"You can forget that. You aren't going anywhere tomorrow. Half past eight. Remember."

Martin and James spent the next day in camp. They had 15 lots of boring jobs to do: clearing, cleaning, tidying. "Most years, everybody in the camp helps with this work," Ms Aston told them. "This year, you're going to do most of it, and you know very well why. Just be glad you're still here. Three years ago, the activity leaders sent two boys and a girl 20 home because they went to pubs."

Martin and James didn't try very hard to be glad, and in the first hour, they didn't try very hard to work. But the activity leaders understood boys very well. "If you can't work alone," Mr Hanbury told them, "one of us will stay with 25 you. All the time."

"It isn't fair," Martin said to James. "We haven't hurt anybody. Who does Ms Aston think she is? Our parents are paying for us here. She can't stop us going riding."

"She *has* stopped us going riding," said James. "And do you 30 really want to explain why to your mum and dad? If we want to do something about it, we've got to think of something else."

That evening, the other three started talking about riding up on the fells. James and Martin did *not* want to hear about 35 it, and started to whisper together.

33

Suddenly, Latif said loudly, "Hey, no, you can't do that!"

"What's wrong, Latif?" asked Sarah. "Who can't do what?"

"I've just heard what these two are planning." Latif pointed at James and Martin and explained to the others.

5 "Oh, please, you two, don't be silly," said Lynn. "If you do that, Ms Aston will know it was you. Then they'll send you home, and I really wouldn't like that."

Lynn smiled at James, and he started to say, "Oh, well, perhaps ..."

10 But Martin stopped him. "Of course she's going to *think* it's us. That's what we want. But she can't *know,* so they can't send us home. And she deserves it."

"You two deserved what you got," said Latif. "You know very well you mustn't drink beer in pubs."

15 "Listen to him!" said Martin, angry now. "You've drunk beer in a pub. You told us."

"Right," said Latif. "And somebody found out. It cost me a month's pocket-money, but I didn't start so say, 'It isn't fair, it isn't fair.' We all like doing things that we mustn't. But if

20 somebody finds out ... Well, you've just got to learn to take it."

"I don't want to listen to this any more," said Martin. "Come on, James, we've got work to do. And you others, don't dare tell anybody."

25 James looked over at Lynn, but he went out with Martin.

"Now what are we going to do?" asked Lynn, who was upset.

"Nothing," answered Sarah. "If we tell Ms Aston, she could send them home. And even if she doesn't, James and

30 Martin won't speak to us again. Martin's right. She can't *know* it's them. Let's just hope nobody finds out."

Martin and James went out into the field behind the camp and found two big, wet cowpats. When they were sure nobody could see them, they brought them into the camp

35 and put them in Ms Aston's bed.

"What a pity we can't watch," said Martin later. "She said beer was smelly. What's she going to think of her bed?"
"Let's go and wash before somebody sees our hands," answered James.

5 In the morning, they weren't so sure about their 'joke' any more. "Do you think they really could send us home?" Martin asked James.
"Don't know," James answered. "Lynn says I deserve it if they do. She's very angry with me."
10 "Yeah, the others just don't think it's funny. – Hmm. Well, we're going to know what's happening soon. Look. There's Ms Aston now, over there."
But Ms Aston just called, "Morning, you two," and walked over to the camp centre.
15 "Somebody told her," said Martin, angry again. "Or they took the cowpats out and cleaned the bed. Wait till we find the others."
"No, leave it, Martin," said James. "I want to be friends with Lynn again. And perhaps it's good that it didn't work. Who
20 knows?"
The programme for the day was rock-climbing on Langdale Pikes, a group of mountains not far from Grasmere. In the bus, Ms Aston was normal and friendly to James. She didn't say a word about cowpats or beds.

"I don't understand it, Martin," whispered James. "Lynn says nobody told Ms Aston and nobody cleaned the bed. So what happened?"

Martin couldn't stop thinking about it. Perhaps that's why the accident happened. They were walking along a narrow path on top of some steep rocks. Martin's head was full of questions about Ms Aston and the cowpats. He wasn't looking at the path or the rocks. Suddenly his feet slid off a rock and he was falling. This time nobody was quick enough to help him.

He fell about three metres onto some grass and started sliding down some scree. He used his hands and feet to try to stop, but it didn't work. At the end of the scree was one very small tree, but it wasn't strong enough to stop Martin. Very, very slowly, it broke. He fell another three or four metres – and stopped at last.

To his surprise, Martin found he could still stand up. "Ow, ow, ow," he thought. "I'm going to be black and blue tomorrow, but I haven't broken anything."

He looked around. "Hmm. I'm all right here, but I can't climb up, and I can't climb down. I'm going to have to wait."

Just then, he heard Ms Aston. "Martin, can you hear me?" she called. Martin answered.

"How badly are you hurt?" Ms Aston called again.

Martin explained. "I'm OK, but I'm very cold," he finished.

"Cold?" asked James. "But it's a hot day. Why is he cold?"

"He's shocked," said Ms Aston. "He needs to have somebody with him."

"Listen, Mike," she said to Mr Hanbury. "I'll go down to him on the rope. When I see what we need, you can send for help. Come on, help me."

"Slowly, slowly, give me some more rope," called Ms Aston. Then, "All right, I can see him now. I'm going over to the right. More rope, slowly–y–y–y– OK. I'm with him."

Ms Aston smiled at Martin. Then she called again: "Mike, he can't climb out of here. I think we're going to have to pull him up. And me, too, probably. We'll need special equipment."

5 "OK, Marion," called Mr Hanbury. "I'll try to be quick."

"Right, Martin," said Ms Aston. "Put these warm clothes on. And here's some soup. Careful, it's hot."

"Thanks," said Martin. "That's better."

"Good," said Ms Aston. "Now we can sit here and wait an 10 hour or two for Mr Hanbury. What are we going to talk about?"

Martin's head was full of thoughts about cowpats. He was beginning to feel very, very bad, but he didn't want to talk about them. So he asked Ms Aston about the camp and the 15 activity leaders. She told him about the others.

After a time, Martin asked, "Why are you a camp activity leader?"

"Because it isn't just hard work, it's fun, too," she answered. "Most of the year, I'm a teacher in London, but I hate the 20 city. I want to be in the countryside, in the mountains. I like the activities that we do here at the camp."

"But you're here all summer," said Martin. "That means you can't go on holiday."

"Oh, there's always Easter," answered Ms Aston. "And if 25 there are no activity leaders, then there are no camps, and no Lake District holidays for people like you and your friends. I like working with young people, too. Even when they go and drink beer in pubs."

Martin felt really bad now. "I've got to say something," he 30 thought. "But how?"

"Ms Aston," he began. She looked at him. "Erm..., when you went to bed last night, did you, erm..., I mean was there anything ...?"

"When I went to bed last night, Martin, I got up again very 35 quickly. Then I needed about half an hour to wash my hair

37

and get clean again. Is that what you wanted to know?"

"Oh no," said Martin. "Oh no. I'm sorry, I'm really sorry. But you see I was so angry and …" He stopped and looked at Ms Aston in surprise. She couldn't stop laughing.

5 "Martin," she said at last. "Of course I knew it was you and James. Who else?"

"But why didn't you say anything? Why weren't you angry?"

"I didn't say anything because that's what you wanted, 10 wasn't it? And when nothing happened, you couldn't understand it, could you? Didn't you and James start to think, 'What's going to happen to us?' Didn't you begin to worry about it?"

"That's right," said Martin. "I couldn't stop thinking about 15 it all morning."

"You see," said Ms Aston, and smiled. "And why wasn't I angry? I'll tell you a story. When I was fourteen, my father found me in a pub with some boys from my school. I was drinking something much stronger than beer, too. Well, 20 the next three weeks I couldn't go out in the evening. Not even to my best friend's house. And I missed a weekend trip to the Welsh mountains with the school. Now, I'm not going to tell you what I did to my father. I don't want to put any dangerous ideas into your head. It worked. It worked 25 too well, and *he* didn't stay quiet about it. But when I saw him I felt terrible."

"Hmm," said Martin. "I feel terrible now."

"Don't," said Ms Aston. "You don't need to." Then, because Martin still looked upset: "Come on, let's enjoy the view. 30 I'm sure you're never going to see the Lake District from here again!"

Before the stories ...

The hike

What are the problems you can have on a hike?
Think about the place, the weather, the people.
Write what you like and don't like about a hike.
What do you need to take with you on a hike?
Think about clothes, food, equipment etc.

It's hotter there

What do some people say about foreigners?
How do they make foreigners feel bad?
Make a list of the special problems for people who look like foreigners e.g. Turks who have grown up in Germany, Pakistanis who have grown up in England.
Think about their life at school, in the street, at home, at the disco, on public transport etc.

The fell race

What do boys think girls can't do or girls aren't good at?
Make a list of five things.
What do girls think boys can't do or boys aren't good at?
Make a list of five things.
Think about jobs, sport, at school, at home, travel etc.

Helvellyn

What problems do tourists bring with them to the places they visit?
Think about noise, rubbish, traffic, graffiti etc.
What special problems do tourists with dogs make?
Can you think of any rules for dogs and their owners in the town and in the countryside?

You get what you deserve

What are the rules in Germany for young people in pubs?

Is it a good idea to have rules about alcohol in public places?
Do you know any rules about alcohol in German shops?
What are the rules about alcohol in your school?
Does the class think it's OK to play a trick on a teacher?

While you are reading the stories ...

The hike

Collect information about the group in this story and the other stories:
Who is the group leader – the strongest person?
Who is the weakest person in the group?
Who is the trouble maker?
Who is the funniest person in the group?
Who is the cleverest person in the group?
Make a list of the problems the group have with their clothes, the hikes, water, their maps, going swimming, their clothes, their leaders etc. at the camp.
Make a list of the things the group liked or enjoyed.

It's hotter there

What words made Latif angry?
How did Latif spend his day?
Find out what Mr Mosely had to do when he heard Latif was missing.
In the evening Mr Mosely said: "… we've got quite a problem in this camp with people who don't think …"
Say what you think Latif did wrong and what Mr Mosely did wrong.

The fell race

Why was Lynn disappointed when they got to Dove Cottage?
Where did Lynn get the idea for a fell race?

Find three problems the runners have in the fell race.

Helvellyn

Why are the mountains in Britain dangerous?
What mistakes did the family from Manchester make on the mountain?
What happened to Martin on Helvellyn?

You get what you deserve

What did Martin and James do wrong?
What were the rules about alcohol in the camp?
What trick did the boys play on Ms Aston?
Why wasn't Ms Aston angry about the cowpats?

After the stories ...

What do you/does the class think?

The hike

Is it OK to write your name on a rock? Say why/why not.

It's hotter there

Did Latif do the right thing when he went off on his own for a day? Say why/why not.

The fell race

Was Clare right to wait for Martin and finish the race with him? Say why/why not.

Helvellyn

Was Ms Morgan fair when she gave the address of the dog owner to the farmer? Say why/why not.

You get what you deserve

Was Ms Aston right to punish the boys? Say why/why not.

Things to do in groups or in class

1. Make a list of all the funny things that happened during the Lake District Camp. Begin like this: *It was funny when …/ I laughed when …/ It was a great joke when …*

2. Make a weather forecast for each day of the camp.
Use the words: *sun, sunny, clouds, cloudy, wind, windy, rain, rainy, warm, hot, temperature, forecast for tomorrow.*
Draw symbols to show the weather, too.

3. William Wordsworth was a famous English poet.
Find out: *when he lived in the Lake District, where he lived, the name of his house and what he wrote about.*
Use your answers to make *part* of a poster about the many interesting things that young people can see and do in the English Lake District.

4. Here's a list of the activities for the children at the Lake District Camp: *hiking, swimming, fell running, map reading, rock-climbing, having a picnic, travelling on a steam train, riding, visiting a museum, watching wrestling, mountain climbing, shopping.*
Put the activities in the order you like best – from 1 to 12.
See what all the class thinks.

5. Plan a week's camp in the country for your class.
Choose the activities, the rules, the food and the place you all want to go to. Make a poster of all your ideas.

Vocabulary

A **alcohol** ['ælkəhɒl] Alkohol
all around [ɔːl ə'raʊnd] ringsum
argument ['ɑːgjʊmənt] Streit, Auseinandersetzung

B **beat** [biːt] schlagen
beer [bɪə] Bier
behave [bɪ'heɪv] sich benehmen, sich verhalten

C **camp site** ['kæmp saɪt] Campingplatz
careful ['keəfəl] vorsichtig
chase [tʃeɪs] jagen
cobweb ['kɒːbweb] Spinnennetz
collar ['kɒlə] Kragen
countryside ['kʌntrɪsaɪd] Landschaft
cowpat ['kaʊpæt] Kuhfladen
cut, cut, cut [kʌt] (sich) schneiden

D **dare** [deə] sich trauen; (es) wagen
deserve [dɪ'zɜːv] verdienen
during ['djʊərɪŋ] während

E **early** ['ɜːlɪ] früh
east [iːst] Ost-; Osten; östlich
equipment [ɪ'kwɪpmənt] Ausrüstung; Geräte

F **farmer** ['fɑːmə] Bauer, Bäuerin
fault [fɔːlt] Schuld, Fehler
fell [fel] Berg; Hochmoor
fire ['faɪə] Brand, Feuer
fit *(adj.)* [fɪt] fit, gut in Form
foot, *pl.* **feet** [fʊt, fiːt] Fuß
foreigner ['fɒrənə] Ausländer, Ausländerin

43

G **get into trouble** ['trʌbl] Ärger bekommen
graffiti [grə'fiːtiː] Graffiti, Wandkritzeleien
grass [grɑːs] Gras
grow up [grəʊ 'ʌp] aufwachsen
gun [gʌn] (Schuß-)Waffe

H **high** [haɪ] hoch
hike [haɪk] Wanderung
hunting ['hʌntɪŋ] (das) Jagen
hurt [hɜːt] (sich) wehtun, (sich) verletzen; verletzt

L **land** [lænd] Land; Grundstück
lazybones ['leɪzɪbəʊnz] Faulpelz
list [lɪst] Liste
lonely ['ləʊnlɪ] einsam, verlassen

M **mad** [mæd] verrückt
minibus ['mɪnɪbʌs] Kleinbus
miss [mɪs] verpassen; vermissen
mood [muːd] Stimmung, Laune
mountainitis [maʊntɪ'naɪtəs] *etwa:* Bergkoller
mountain ['maʊntɪn] Berg
mountain rescue ['maʊntɪn 'reskjuː] Bergwacht

N **narrow** ['nærəʊ] eng, schmal
nasty ['nɑːstɪ] gemein
nuclear reprocessing plant ['njuːklɪə rɪ'prəʊsesɪŋ plɑːnt]
atomare Wiederaufbereitungsanlage

O **orienteering** [ɔːrɪən'tɪərɪŋ] Orientierungslauf (mit
Karte und Kompaß)
own: on his/her own [əʊn] alleine

P **Paki** ['pækɪ] *(Schimpfwort)* Pakistaner, Pakistanerin
path [pɑːθ] (Fuß-)Weg

44

pay, paid, paid [peɪ, peɪd] (be)zahlen
peace [piːs] Frieden
person [ˈpɜːsn] Mensch, Person
pick up [ˈpɪk ˈʌp] aufheben, hochheben
plastic bag [ˈplæstɪk ˈbæg] Plastiktüte
poem [ˈpəʊɪm] Gedicht
poet [ˈpəʊɪt] Dichter, Dichterin
pub [pʌb] Gaststätte, Kneipe
public: public transport [pʌblɪk ˈtrænspɔːt] öffentliche
   Verkehrsmittel
punish [ˈpʌnɪʃ] bestrafen

R rights [raɪts] Rechte, Bürgerrechte
rope [rəʊp] Seil
rubbish [ˈrʌbɪʃ] Unsinn; Abfall
rucksack [ˈrʌksæk] Rucksack
rule [ruːl] Regel, Vorschrift

S scree [skriː] Schutthalde; Geröll
sheep [ʃiːp] Schaf, Schafe
sheepdog trials [ˈʃiːpdɒg traɪəlz] Schäferhund-
   prüfungen
shocked [ʃɒkt] schockiert, bestürzt
shoot, shot, shot [ʃuːt, ʃɒt] (er)schießen
side [saɪd] Seite
slide, slid, slid [slaɪd, slɪd] rutschen
sometime [ˈsʌmtaɪm] irgendwann
son [sʌn] Sohn
spoil [spɔɪl] verderben, verschandeln
steam [stiːm] Dampf
steam train [ˈstiːm treɪn] Dampfeisenbahn
steep [stiːp] steil
stone [stəʊn] Stein
story, stories [ˈstɔːrɪ(z)] Erzählung(en), Geschicht(en)
stream [striːm] Wasserlauf, Bach

45

strong [strɒŋ] stark, heftig
stupid ['stjuːpɪd] dumm, blöd

T **traffic** ['træfɪk] Verkehr
trick: play a trick [trɪk] einen Streich spielen
trouble ['trʌbl] Ärger
Turk [tɜːk] Türke, Türkin

U **upset** [ʌp'set] durcheinander, aufgeregt, betrübt

V **view** [vjuː] Aussicht, Blick

W **water** ['wɔːtə] Wasser
weak [wiːk] schwach
whisper ['wɪspə] flüstern
whistle ['wɪsəl] (das) Pfeifen
wild [waɪəld] wild; stürmisch
wind [wɪnd] Wind
wrestling ['resəlɪŋ] Ringen
wrong: do wrong [rɒŋ] falsch handeln

Place names

Aberdeen [æbə'di:n]
Beacon Park ['bi:kən 'pɑːk]
Blea Tarn ['bliː 'tɑːn]
Boot [buːt]
Cockly Beck ['kɒklɪ 'bek]
Coniston ['kɒnɪstən]
Dalegarth ['deɪlgɑːθ]
Dove Cottage [dʌv 'kɒtɪdʒ]
Eskdale ['eskdeɪəl]
Glenridding [glen'rɪdɪŋ]
Grasmere ['grɑːsmɪə]
Halifax ['hælɪfæks]
Hardknott Pass
 ['hɑːdnɒt 'pɑːs]
Helvellyn [hel'velɪn]
Lake District ['leɪk dɪstrɪkt]
Langdale Pikes
 ['læŋdeɪl 'paɪks]

Manchester ['mæntʃɪstə]
Ravenglass Railway
 ['reɪvənglɑːs 'reɪəlweɪ]
Red Tarn [red 'tɑːn]
Red Tarn Beck [red tɑːn 'bek]
River Duddon ['rɪvə 'dʌdən]
River Esk ['rɪvər 'esk]
River Mite ['rɪvə 'maɪt]
Sellafield ['seləfɪːld]
Striding Edge ['straɪdɪŋ 'edʒ]
Swansea ['swɒnzɪ]
Thirlmere ['θɜːlmɪə]
Ullswater ['ʌlzwɔːtə]
Wast Water ['wɒst wɔːtə]
Wrynose Bottom
 ['raɪnəuz 'bɒtəm]
Wrynose Pass ['raɪnəuz 'pɑːs]

Other names

Aston ['æstən]
Hanbury ['hænbərɪ]
Morgan ['mɔːgən]

Mosely ['məuzlɪ]
William Wordsworth
 ['wɪljəm 'wɜːdzwəθ]

47